W9-AYK-897

WHY DOES MY BODY MAKE BUBBLES?

Learning about the Digestive System with

THE GARBAGE GANG

by Thomas Kingsley Troupe

Illustrated by Derek Toye

PICTURE WINDOW BOOKS
a capstone imprint

MEET THE GARBAGE GANG:

SAM HAMMWICH

Sam is a once-delicious sandwich that has a bit of lettuce and tomato. He is usually crabby and a bit of a loudmouth.

GORDY

Gordy is a small rhino who wears an eyepatch even though he doesn't need one. He lives in the city dump. His friends don't visit him in the smelly dump, so Gordy created his own friends—the Garbage Gang!

SOGGY

Soggy is a stuffed bear from a carnival game. She fell into a puddle of dumpster juice and has never been the same.

RICK

Rick is a brick. He is terrified of bugs, especially bees, which is odd . . . since he's a brick.

CANN-DEE

Cann-Dee is a robot made of aluminum cans. She can pull random facts out of thin air.

MR. FRIGID

Mr. Frigid is a huge refrigerator that sprouted arms and legs. He doesn't say much, but he's super strong.

At Gordy's home in the city garbage dump ...

It doesn't matter how much you scrub, Gordy. The dump's stink never comes off.

A little more soap, and I should be just fine.

That's what you think, kid. Embrace the stink!

I fell in dumpster juice once. I've been smelly ever since.

Did you really just come out of my body?

I sure did!

Please don't pop! Please don't pop!

So, why do I have gas coming out of me?

There are a whole lot of reasons, Gordy. One of the big reasons is that bacteria live inside your body, in your intestines. Gas is produced when bacteria digest food.

So it's ... bacteria? Inside Gordy?
Yes, but sometimes gas forms when you swallow too much air.
Please cut down on the air you swallow, Gordy.
Research data indicates that people pass gas 13 to 20 times per day. Everyone does it.
Not me. I'm a sandwich, not a gassy rhinoceros!
Actually, bacteria are ON you, Sam. We can't see them, but they're breaking you down and making gas. So you smell on the outside!
Rye, I oughta ...

The small intestine! It breaks down the food even further. Then it absorbs proteins, vitamins, minerals, and other stuff in food. A human's small intestine is up to 22 feet (6.7 meters) long.

That seems long. Who's the pickle-head who decided to call it the small intestine?

I think the name means the opening is small.

It's small alright! Ugh, I feel like I've been slimed!

That slime comes from the liver and pancreas. The liver provides bile, and the pancreas provides enzymes to help break down food.

liver

stomach

pancreas

large intestine

small intestine

anus

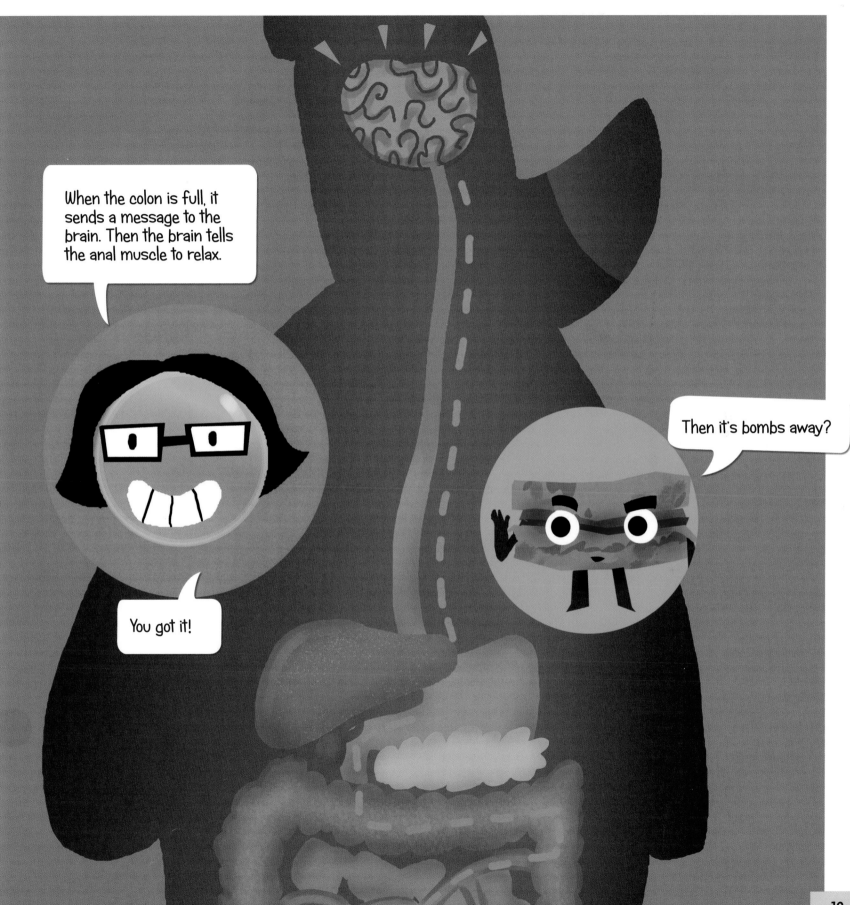

I'm afraid to ask, but why does poop stink, and why is it brown?
The bacteria in the food and the chemicals they create make it extra stinky. It's the same stuff that makes gas bubbles like me smell so good!
Accessing database. Feces gets its brown color from bilirubin. Bilirubin is a brown substance in bile that comes from the liver.

Glossary

anus—the lower opening of the digestive system; solid wastes move out of the body through the anus

bacteria—very small living things that exist all around you and inside you; some bacteria cause disease

bile—green or yellow liquid that helps with digestion

colon—the main part of the large intestine that absorbs water and other parts of food that have not digested

digest—to break down food so the body can use it

enzyme—a protein that makes chemical changes to food

intestine—a long organ that carries and digests food and stores waste products; it is divided into the small intestine and large intestine

mineral—a material found in nature that is not an animal or plant

nutrients—parts of food, like vitamins, that are used for growth

protein—a particle of food needed to keep the body healthy

vitamin—a nutrient that helps keep people healthy

You're looking up words? That's one smart move, kid!

Read More

Gold, Susan Dudley. *Learning About the Digestive and Excretory Systems.* Berkeley Heights, N.J.: Enlsow, Publishers, 2013.

Kolpin, Molly. *A Tour of Your Digestive System.* Body Systems. North Mankato, Minn.: Capstone Press, 2013.

Royston, Angela. *Puke and Poo.* Disgusting Body Facts. Chicago: Raintree, 2010.

My sensors indicate that books about the digestive system do not stink.

Critical Thinking Using the Common Core

1. What happens to food when it enters the stomach? (Key Ideas and Details)

2. What happens in the large intestine? (Key Ideas and Details)

Index

Internet Sites

FactHound offers a safe, fun way to find Internet sites related to this book. All of the sites on FactHound have been researched by our staff.

Here's all you do:

Visit www.facthound.com

Type in this code: 9781479554805

Super-cool stuff!

Check out projects, games and lots more at
www.capstonekids.com

Thanks to our advisers for their expertise, research, and advice:
Christopher T. Ruhland, PhD
Professor of Biological Sciences
Department of Biology
Minnesota State University, Mankato

Terry Flaherty, PhD, Professor of English
Minnesota State University, Mankato

Editor: Shelly Lyons
Designer: Lori Bye
Art Director: Nathan Gassman
Production Specialist: Gene Bentdahl
The illustrations in this book were created digitally.

Picture Window Books are published by Capstone,
1710 Roe Crest Drive, North Mankato, Minnesota 56003
www.capstonepub.com

Library of Congress Cataloging-in-Publication Data
Troupe, Thomas Kingsley, author.
Why does my body make bubbles? : learning about the digestive system with the garbage gang? / by Thomas Kingsley Troupe ; illustrated by Derek Toye. pages cm. — (Nonfiction picture books. The garbage gang's super science questions)
Audience: 5-7.
Audience: K to grade 3.
 Summary: "Humorous text and characters teach kids all about the human digestive system"— Provided by publisher.
ISBN 978-1-4795-5480-5 (library binding)
ISBN 978-1-4795-5488-1 (eBook PDF)
1. Digestive organs—Juvenile literature. 2. Stomach—Juvenile literature. 3. Intestines—Juvenile literature. I. Toye, Derek, illustrator. II. Title.
QM301.T76 2015
612.3—dc23   2014001537

Printed in the United States of America in
North Mankato, Minnesota.
032014   008087CGF14

More books!!!! Are you kidding me? This is the best news since sliced bread!

Seriously?

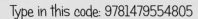

Look for all the books in the series:

DO ANTS GET LOST? Learning about Animal Communication with **THE GARBAGE GANG**

DO BEES POOP? Learning about Living and Nonliving Things with **THE GARBAGE GANG**

WHY DO DEAD FISH FLOAT? Learning about Matter with **THE GARBAGE GANG**

WHY DOES MY BODY MAKE BUBBLES? Learning about the Digestive System with **THE GARBAGE GANG**